About the Author

Peter Denison was commissioned from the Royal Military Academy, Sandhurst, into the Duke of Edinburgh's Royal Regiment. He resigned his commission in the rank of Captain in order to commence training as a probation officer: he remained in the Probation Service for thirty-seven years. After becoming a Christian in 1974, he was involved in various Christian offender rehabilitation related charities, including the Probation Service Christian Fellowship (National Chairman), Prison Fellowship (South East England Coordinator) and Stepping Stones Trust (SST Chairman for twenty-eight years), receiving an OBE for his work in SST. He has a passionate interest in seeing the Lord at work in the lives of prisoners. Married for fifty-two years, he and his wife live in West Sussex.

Freedom for Prisoners

Peter Denison

Freedom for Prisoners

Olympia Publishers
London

www.olympiapublishers.com
OLYMPIA PAPERBACK EDITION

A CIP catalogue record for this title is
available from the British Library.

ISBN: 978-1-80074-245-1

First Published in 2021

Olympia Publishers
Tallis House
2 Tallis Street
London
EC4Y 0AB

Printed in Great Britain

Acknowledgements

My thanks to Rev Tom Robson, Vicar of All Saints, Wick (Littlehampton), for encouraging me to write Christian articles and also to Peter Flower and Lorna Windmill, who have been such an inspiration to me.

I am also grateful to my wife, who showed such patience, while I was writing this book.

Michael and Caroline,

I appreciate the way you have both encouraged and led the Baker family.

Every blessing,

Peter   29.10.21.

Foreword for Freedom for Prisoners by Jonathan Aitken

Peter Denison's *Freedom for Prisoners* is a book of inspirational spiritual excellence. It combines the finest gems from the author's personal witness, teachings and experiences at the sharp end of Prison Ministry.

I am delighted, but not entirely surprised, by Peter's late in life emergence as a distinguished Christian author, for he has devoted most of his career to serving God within the fraternity of fallen ex-offenders.

For thirty-five years Peter was a full time Probation Officer which he combined with Chairing the Probation Service Christian Fellowship. He also served for twenty-eight years as Chair of the Stepping Stones Trust, an innovative South London housing and mentoring charity which cared for over seventy ex-prisoners.

Having seen Peter in action in prison chapels and at Stepping Stones Trust (where his work was recognised by the Honour of an OBE) I know that he is an outstanding Christian public servant of great wisdom and experience in the specialised field of ministering to ex-offenders.

The book is a collection of short talks given by Peter to prisoners about the main elements of the Christian faith. The talks are packed with some interesting, spiritual insights. Bible scriptures are quoted in full, as Peter rightly believes that the Holy Spirit can powerfully 'speak' through the scriptures. I recommend this book, written in a direct and punchy style, coupled with an infectious zeal for God's truths.

Books 'hold one's attention' if they are relevant to our personal situation: having recently had two near death experiences, as a result of Covid and heart attacks, the chapters on Covid, worry and prayer were particularly apposite for me.

'Revival' is an imaginative chapter quoting a fictitious testimony (during the time of Jesus), of an Egyptian Jew visiting Jerusalem for the Passover Feast and staying on until Pentecost.

The chapter, 'How and Why I came to Earth?' reveals Peter's questioning stance to life: this and a few other chapters are relevant to those who, during these uncertain times, are seeking to understand the purpose of life.

Freedom for Prisoners aims to stimulate those with no faith into seeking answers to life. It should also be of interest to Christians, in particular the last two chapters about Christian counselling, which cover how to become a Christian and baptism in the Spirit.

Over the years, there has been some growing interest in the role of Christianity in the prisons. I have found this to be true in my current role as a Chaplain in Pentonville Prison. As a result of the pandemic a desire to discover God has increased. The book assists in this search because it concentrates on the importance of understanding Christian truths.

Peter's second book, *Freedom in Christ* will shortly be published by Olympia Publishers and concentrates on the Gospel of Christ, including prisoners' testimonies of change, as a result of their 'new lives' in Christ.

I am sure these books will be an inspiration to the spiritual lives of both prisoners and ex-prisoners. There are few individuals who have the breadth, knowledge and understanding that Peter Denison has in this field. His writings are, and will surely continue to be, a new addition to this important, but far too often ignored, area of Christian Ministry.

Jonathan Aitken
22 June 2021

Contents

Chapter 1 Witness 15

Chapter 2 Talks to Prisoners 23

Chapter 3 Fundamental Elements of the Christian Faith .27

Chapter 4 Oaks of Righteousness 33

Chapter 5 The Invisible Fight for the Heart 36

Chapter 6 How and why did I come into this world? 39

Chapter 7 Pentecostal Revival 45

Chapter 8 Philippians and Prisoners 53

Chapter 9 Judgement Day 57

Chapter 10 Prayer, Worry and Anxiety 62

Chapter 11 A New and Living Way 66

Chapter 12 Our Light and Momentary Trials 71

Chapter 13 Christ in you, the Hope of Glory 75

Chapter 14 Why Covid? 79

Chapter 15 Christian Counselling 85

Chapter 16 Counselling a Believer in the Baptism of the Holy Spirit 90

Chapter 1
Witness

I have only had two jobs. My first was an Army Officer. After being commissioned from the Royal Military Academy Sandhurst, I joined an infantry regiment, serving for six years until, as a Captain, I decided to resign my commission in order to train as a probation officer. Having qualified as a probation officer, I remained in this work for thirty-five years.

I will cover three areas of my life:
> **Becoming a Christian**
> **Experiences and views of the Probation Service**
> **Involvement with Christian offender rehabilitation charities**

1. Becoming a Christian

1) In 1974, I became a Christian, which was a life changing experience. Hitherto I had been a churchgoer but while training at Bristol University I formed a friendship with a fellow trainee, who was a Christian: I realized that his faith was much deeper than mine and so started exploring Christianity.

2) During this period, I felt the Lord showed me the addictive nature of sin. I had inherited some money and started 'gambling' on the stock market. In due course, I felt strongly convicted by Christ's words, '*Where your treasure*

is, there will your heart be also' (Matthew 6:21). My slavish heart was in the stock market, from which I wanted to be freed.

3) After a service at Halford House Christian Fellowship in Richmond, Surrey, I repented of my sins, especially gambling, and asked Christ into my life: He came in, changed me and became my Lord and Saviour.

4) Four years later, in 1978, I was baptised in the Holy Spirit, who empowered me for ministry with offenders.

2. **Experiences and views of the Probation Service.**

1) Working as a probation officer was fascinating work, particularly in the early years. I felt an affinity with prisoners and offenders, many of whom, according to one of my former clients, had been 'dealt a bad set of cards in life.'

2) When I started in 1971 the penal system was very different from what it is now. One of my first clients, whom I visited in prison, told me that, when arrested for killing a four-year-old child, he expected to be hung as he had not realized that capital punishment had recently been abolished. In fact, his and a similar sexually motivated offence by another offender were subsequently debated in parliament, nearly resulting in the restoration of capital punishment.

3) Years ago, as probation officers, we took greater risks than would currently be acceptable. For instance, I allowed a few homeless clients to stay in our home, with my wife and three small children.

4) We experienced violence in the workplace. In Richmond Probation Office (the first office in which I

worked), out of five officers, three were assaulted. I was hit a couple of times. My senior was held hostage for four hours, with a broken bottle against his throat, while Arthur Caiger, a Christian colleague and 'spiritual father' to me, had acid thrown into his eyes and never recovered his sight. Arthur forgave the assailant, although the latter was never caught.

3. In 1907 the Service was formed out of the Police Court Mission. The Christian emphasis was continued through the Probation Service Christian Fellowship (PSCF), which changed its name to Christians in Probation.

1) From 1981 — 1988 I was the National Chairman of PSCF, which provided probation staff support through house parties, prayer groups and newsletters. The Fellowship encountered difficulties in seeking to uphold the Christian ethos.

2) When I left the Probation Service in 2006 the main emphasis was on the enforcement of community orders, prison licences and parole. I felt that while enforcement was vital, it should not mask the equally important task of probation officers seeking to build meaningful relationships with their clients.

3) There are three important elements in potentially successful work with offenders — these are accommodation, employment and motivation. The most important of these three elements is motivation to change, which I frequently saw in those who, as a result of embracing a deep, intimate, personal relationship with the Lord Jesus Christ, accepted and followed the moral code of the Christian faith and consequently kept out of trouble.

4) During the day I worked as a full-time probation officer, while in the evenings, I was heavily involved with Christian offender rehabilitation charities.

4. Involvement with Christian Rehabilitation Charities

1) A year after being baptised in the Holy Spirit, I became the first Prison Fellowship Regional Co-ordinator, with my main task being to set up prayer groups for the London Prisons: subsequently my post was expanded to cover South East England.

2) One of our prayer groups was run by Christian prison officers from Ashford Remand Centre. The local press called them, 'the God Squad': they circulated and marked Christian correspondence courses for 1000 young offenders in the remand centre.

3) Many different churches and denominations were involved, including HTB, Brompton.

5. Prison Fellowship had an interesting early history

1) In 1974 in America a man called Chuck Colson was imprisoned for his part in the Watergate Scandal: he had been President Nixon's Special Counsel. Whilst serving his sentence, Chuck became a Christian and soon afterwards developed a friendship, through correspondence, with a British Christian politician, Michael Alison, who had a similar political role in the U.K. — at the time he was Prime Minister Margaret Thatcher's Parliamentary Private Secretary.

2) Subsequently, Michael's wife became the leader of the newly formed Prison Christian Fellowship in the UK. It

was supported by Chuck Colson, who set up the first Prison Fellowship in America.

3) I met some interesting, florid offenders whilst in Prison Fellowship. One was Brian Greenaway, who became a Christian while serving a long sentence at Dartmoor Prison for brutal crimes committed while president of a Hell's Angel Chapter.

4) After his release, Brian became a Prison Evangelist and London City Mission asked me to supervise his work as a prison evangelist. Brian managed to obtain entry into half the prisons in the country. On one occasion he visited Strangeways Prison, in Manchester, and spoke to a gathering of a thousand prisoners. Many prisoners became Christians through Brian's ministry, which was enhanced through two books he wrote about his life.

6. I saw mini revivals in several prisons. As an example, in Strangeways Prison there were three Sunday morning services (the first two being full) to cater for the large number of prisoners wanting to attend chapel — a third of the prisoners in the establishment. In this and other prisons the Holy Spirit was challenging prisoners, who while in custody had plenty of time to consider the deep questions in life, especially those in regard to personal faith:

1) The most significant crime causation statement ever made is recorded in Mark 7:21 when the Lord Jesus Christ said, '*For from within, out of men's hearts, come evil thoughts, sexual immorality, theft, murder, adultery, greed, malice, deceit...*[1] '

---

[1] All scripture quotations in this book are taken from the *Life Application Bible (New International Version)*, Kingsway Publications,

2) As crimes originate from the heart, what is required is a 'spiritual heart transplant,' through faith in Christ. While several prisoners make Christian commitments, some do not fully understand what they are doing, others just use the Christian label, while a number are sincere.

3) The difficulty we used to find was to encourage prisoners to maintain their positive resolve on release. Many soon forget about their 'brush' with Christianity. To support ex-prisoners on release, a couple of us felt the need to provide Christian homes, catering for released prisoners, who had become Christians while in custody.

7. Consequently, in 1984 we decided to establish a new charity, called 'Stepping Stones Trust', in order to provide Christian support and accommodation for ex-prisoners:

1) We opened our first hostel in Wandsworth. Gradually the work grew in the London area, so that by the time we handed over our operations to a larger charity in 2012, we were catering for seventy-two ex-prisoners in large and small hostels, as well as providing them with 'move-on' flats. All this was done in a Christian context, with links to supportive churches in London.

2) In addition to providing accommodation, we also had a full-time team in Wormwood Scrubs, as well as in Brixton Prison, where we had over seventy volunteers, mainly from local black-led churches. For a short period, we also worked in Belmarsh high security prison.

3) Stepping Stones Trust's patron was Jonathan Aitken, who still comments on TV about Criminal Justice matters. Jonathan started life with many advantages and

---

Eastbourne, 1988.

eventually became a cabinet minister. It was while he was in prison that the Lord 'ignited' his Christian faith.

8. One of the drawbacks of conventional ex-offender hostels is that on leaving a hostel often clients do not have much support, whereas in Stepping Stones Trust we tried to provide ongoing support:

1) For instance, one of our clients, with whom we were in contact for ten years, had committed a number of offences, usually under the influence of alcohol. Having become a Christian in one of our hostels, he was linked with a local church, where he became the curate. He was later ordained and took on a parish.

2) While there he returned to heavy drinking and was placed in custody in Brixton Prison, where he hung himself. The lesson from this is the importance of true repentance and renouncing of past addictions, otherwise the 'tentacles' of these addictions can subsequently re-emerge with disastrous consequences.

3) Although we had some failures, we also had some success. As Chairman of Stepping Stones Trust for twenty-eight years, when I received an OBE for this work, the Queen was particularly interested in our specialist hostel for sex offenders, catering for paedophiles and rapists. She was pleasantly surprised when I told her that over the eighteen years this small hostel had been in operation, none of the residents had been reconvicted for sex offences.

9. Currently, I attend Sunday morning services on a fortnightly basis in a prison, where I enjoy fellowship with other believers. Probation Officers in the early 1970's

hardly ever came across Christian prisoners. However, over the years there has been a gradual, steady increase in interest amongst prisoners in Christianity. I have been privileged in seeing the Lord fulfilling His ministry (described in Luke 4:16-21) in bringing spiritual freedom to prisoners, who appear to demonstrate a greater desire and 'thirst' to know Christ than those 'outside' in the community.

Chapter 2
Talks to Prisoners

Salvation for Prisoners

1. God appears to have a special affection for prisoners, who have plenty of time to think about life. A number start wondering about whether or not there is a God and if there is, what does He want of them?

2. Psalm 107 describes how God rescues those who seek His assistance in desperate circumstances. The psalm describes the plight of four types of people in distress and how God rescues them — wanderers, the sick, the storm-tossed and verses 10 to 16 of this psalm describe experiences of prisoners.

3. Verse 10 refers to prisoners: '*Some sat in darkness and the deepest gloom.*' Understandably, 'deepest gloom' (depression) is a common experience for prisoners. Verse 14: '*He brought them out of darkness and the deepest gloom and broke away their chains.*' It is important that on becoming a Christian there is a clear renunciation and turning away from the 'harmful tentacles of addictions', such as gambling, pornography, alcohol and drugs. If this fails to happen, sometimes many years later, satanic powers have a nasty habit of seeking to tempt people back to former addictions.

4. Verse 13: '*Then they cried to the Lord in their trouble, and he saved them from their distress.*' They suddenly begin to think positively, as if a light of understanding had been switched on in their minds by the Holy Spirit. When a desperate person genuinely turns to God, it is nearly always as a result of God's urging. Christ describes it this way (John 6:44), '*No-one can come to me unless the Father who sent me draws him.*' God, not man, plays the most active role in salvation. When someone chooses to believe in Jesus Christ as Saviour, he or she does so only in response to the urging of the Holy Spirit. God does the urging; then we decide whether or not to believe.

5. Quite a few prisoners have told me of past significant encounters with God when they have cried out to Him in desperation. Their cries to God have often been similar, so I have called them the 'Prisoner's Prayer,' which is nearly always said by depressed and sometimes suicidal prisoners. This simple prayer is, "If there is a God, please help me," with the result that they suddenly become aware of the presence of God — in similar circumstances to the experiences of the prisoners described in Psalm 107. Here are a few points about the 'Prisoner's Prayer':-

1) It is the most effective prayer I know. While God does not delight in our difficulties, because He is a God of love, He does know that it is vital for people to be challenged by the gospel of Christ, who came to this Earth to bring forgiveness of sin and reconciliation with God. We tend to become more open and responsive to God when in difficulties.

2) Mothers are so close to their babies that they can discern the difference between an attention-seeking cry from one of desperation. In the same way, God is attuned to us and responds in love to those who genuinely appeal to Him.

3) An interesting feature about this prayer is that it starts with the words, 'If there is a God,' so the prisoner does not even know if God exists. This should be an encouragement to those who think that they must have a full knowledge of Christian doctrine before asking Christ to become their Lord. Whilst it is important to understand the essence of the Christian faith before responding to the gospel, in special, life-threatening circumstances it seems that God is prepared to waive this requirement by responding in loving acceptance to those who cry out to Him in desperation.

4) I met a prisoner who told me that while in solitary confinement he prayed the 'Prisoner's Prayer' and subsequently was so moved by the presence of God that he became a Christian. He was visited six months later by a Christian probation officer colleague of mine. The latter was amazed at the change in the prisoner, who had spiritually grown over the six months that he spent in 'solitary confinement.'

5) The prisoner saw virtually no-one during this period so could only have acquired his intimate knowledge of the Lord through the inspiration of the Holy Spirit guiding him through the Bible, which he had been given. The man would get up in the early hours of the morning to fast and pray, mainly for others in the prison. On release, he and his wife slept on the floor, as the prisoner felt he had to give away

his bed, which he had obtained through ill-gotten gains. He subsequently worked for a Christian charity providing support and accommodation for released prisoners.

6) God's timing is perfect — he draws us to Jesus at just the right time. This is often when we are under pressure, depressed and able to recognize that our own personal resources are insufficient to cope: it is usually at this stage that we turn to God for help.

7) Many years ago, I visited a prisoner in a London prison. He was on remand in custody on a murder charge. Whilst on this period of remand he became a Christian. Two weeks later he was released on bail, during which time he himself was murdered. God, in His mercy, had given the prisoner a 'narrow window of opportunity' to respond to His call to repentance and faith.

Chapter 3
Fundamental Elements of the Christian Faith

1. It is important to see how the fundamental elements of the Christian faith combine together to form the gospel: these elements include sin, the love and judgement of God the Father, Christ's ministry on Earth, the importance of the Cross, repentance, resurrection, ascension, new birth and the Holy Spirit — quite a lot to cover in ten minutes.

2. God made Adam and Eve in His own image so that He could live with humanity for ever in harmony. He created the Garden of Eden, with a tree from which Adam and Eve were told that they could not eat. God wanted them to obey, but gave them the freedom of choice, without which they would have just been automatons, showing unthinking, hollow obedience.

3. In Genesis 2:16 and 17, God said, '*You are free to eat from any tree in the garden but you must not eat from the tree of the knowledge of good and evil, for when you eat of it you will surely die.*' Adam and Eve did eat from it, with the result that God judged them (Genesis 3:19), '*By the sweat of your brow you will eat your food until you return to the ground, since from it you were taken; for dust you are and to dust you will return.*' In other words, God told them

they would die and so they did both physically and spiritually. As a result of Adam and Eve's disobedience the whole human race inherited a natural tendency to sin. This was exacerbated because humanity came under the deceitful and sinful influence of Satan, who was at war with God.

4. Despite the sinful condition of the human race, God had a plan to redeem humanity. God's love is clearly seen in His dealings with the Children of Israel — His chosen race, who constantly tested Him. They had a rebellious and disobedient attitude towards God, who nevertheless lavished spiritual and physical provisions upon them. His love for them sometimes involved judgement on their wayward behaviour and twice he banished them to foreign lands (Assyria and Babylon).

5. The state of mankind has not changed much since then. We think that our great knowledge, scientific achievements, and civilization provide us greater understanding than our forebears. In fact, humanity's achievements don't significantly improve our circumstances because most still ignore the God who created them: this is because we have a sinful, selfish heart, which is opposed to God.

6. Some parts of the Bible are mysterious — such as God's approach to our sin. God did not decide to send His Son into the world in response to Adam's disobedience, as He had already decided on this plan before the creation of the world. God's plan was that as sin entered the world

through one man, Adam, it therefore had to be a man, albeit a sinless Man, who would take the punishment of the sins of the whole world. The Lord Jesus Christ, who was fully man and fully God (although He left some of His divine attributes in heaven) took our sin on Himself.

7. The culmination of Christ's ministry was His sacrificial death on the Cross: the beneficiaries would be humanity, as well as God. The sin of humanity was placed on the Lord and this satisfied the wrath of God against sin, retaining God's law that states that sin deserves the punishment of death. The Lord's last words on the Cross were, "It is finished." By this He meant that the sin question had been answered in His death — sin and Satan were defeated at the Cross.

8. For forty days after Our Lord's resurrection, He taught His disciples. In one of his last talks (Acts 1:4-8) He commanded his disciples to wait for 'the promise of the Father,' referring to the Holy Spirit. He had prophesied that the Spirit would empower the disciples to be witnesses to His ministry. The reason for a few days' delay after Christ's ascension, before the outpouring of the Spirit at Pentecost, was to give God the Father time to confirm His acceptance of His Son's sacrifice for the sin of the whole world. At Pentecost God, the Father, revealed His satisfaction with His Son's sacrifice by pouring out the Holy Spirit, who empowered the disciples to witness very effectively: within a few days there were three thousand Christians.

9. Humanity is currently in a state of spiritual warfare

— Satan, the god of this world, has blinded the minds of unbelievers to the reality of God. We have a natural aptitude for sin — the Bible says that we are sinful from birth. James 4:1-3 explains how we fight and quarrel because of our sinful desires battling within us.

10. What are we to do? For believers we need to draw closer to the Lord. For unbelievers the first step is to acknowledge that we are sinners. It is only then that we can recognize that we need a Saviour. Some find sin a hard concept and tend to think of it mainly in terms of criminal convictions.

11. When Our Lord was asked which was the greatest commandment, He said it was, '*Love the Lord your God with all your heart and with all your soul and with all your mind.*' (Matthew 22:37). It is only after we love God that He enables us to love our neighbour as ourselves. The point is that from God's perspective all who do not place Him first in their lives are sinners, as God's first command is to love Him. The Church of England describes the chief aim of Man being, 'to glorify God.'

12. Therefore, an unbeliever needs to repent of sin, believe in Christ and receive Him as Lord and Saviour. If God accepts this as a genuine desire for change and consequently gives new (spiritual) life, we become aware of the Holy Spirit's presence in our lives. God moves us from the dominion of sin, Satan and darkness into the dominion and rule of Christ. Moving out of sin's domain does not mean that we never sin again but it does mean that

we are no longer in slavery to sin. Through the ministry of the Holy Spirit we need to be quick to repent of outstanding sin and continue to develop a deep, personal relationship with Our Lord.

13. The Christian discovers that the Bible is a life-giving book and we naturally seek out fellowship with other Christians, all wanting to learn more about the Lord. There will be plenty of opposition, sometimes even from within our own families, who do not understand our change of life. The Bible explains the reason for Christians being misunderstood in 1 Corinthians 2:14: *'The man without the Spirit (the unbeliever) does not accept the things that come from the Spirit of God, for they are foolishness to him, and he cannot understand them, because they are spiritually discerned.'*

14. Judgement is one of the fundamental elements of the Christian Faith. All, whether Christian or not, will one day stand before the Judgement Seat of Christ. We will be judged on our conduct here on Earth: Christ indicated that His main criteria will be the quality of our relationship with Him. He said (Matthew 7:22-23), *'Many will say to me on that day (judgement), 'Lord, Lord did we not prophesy in your name, and in your name drive out demons and perform many miracles?' Then I will tell them plainly, 'I never knew you. Away from me, you evildoers!'*' Judging from the Christian terminology used by those to whom Christ referred, they seemed to be churchgoers, but that was not Christ's primary concern — which was whether or not they had a personal relationship with Him. When Christ prayed

to His Father He said (John 17:3), '*Now this is life eternal: that they may know you, the only true God, and Jesus Christ, whom you have sent.*'

15. Genesis chapter 2 refers to the Tree of Life, which was in the centre of the Garden of Eden and Adam was not allowed to eat from that tree. In Genesis 3, after Adam's disobedience, God said that he and Eve would be prevented from taking fruit from the Tree of Life. However, at the end of the Bible (in Revelation chapter 22) the redeemed of the Lord are allowed to take from the Tree of Life. Our eternal destiny depends on whether or not we want to seek out, discover and know the living Lord Jesus.

Chapter 4
Oaks of Righteousness

1. **Isaiah 61.** About seven hundred and thirty years before the birth of Christ, Isaiah wrote this prophecy. Jesus read from this chapter when he attended a synagogue: *'The Spirit of the Lord is on me because he has anointed me to preach good news to the poor. He has sent me to proclaim freedom for the prisoners and recovery of sight for the blind, to release the oppressed, to proclaim the year of the Lord's favour'* (Luke 4:18).

2. **Poor and Oppressed.** Jesus described those to whom He would preach — 'the poor, prisoners, blind and oppressed.' The 'poor and oppressed' describe many in prison today. Jesus was proclaiming that He was the One who would provide liberty to the physical and spiritual captives. Christ did not come for those who felt they were wise, learned theologians and famous, but to the humble, meek and obedient, who in faith received his message of salvation.

3. **Third world Countries.** Christ is the same today as He was during His earthly ministry. He still seems to focus on the vulnerable and poor. Today third world countries, where there are often many vulnerable and poor people, are currently experiencing great spiritual revivals, while

European countries, like the U.K., appear to be 'spiritually dry.'

4. **Desperate Plea.** Christ eagerly looks for those who are genuinely interested in His message, whether or not they have a good understanding of the Bible. I have heard a number of testimonies from prisoners, who in desperation have just cried out to God with these words, 'If there is a God, please help me.' Like a mother, who can discern the difference between her child's attention seeking cry from one of desperation, God knows our hearts and loves to manifest Himself by helping people in desperate situations.

5. **Oaks of Righteousness.** God wants us to become strong in our faith. Isaiah 61: 3 describes those to whom He gives His favour as 'Oaks of Righteousness.' An oak is comprised of durable, hard wood that can last for centuries. As believers, the Holy Spirit enables us to become steadfast, faithful believers, described here as 'Oaks of Righteousness', receiving the following blessings, listed in verse 3, *'to comfort all who mourn, and provide for those who grieve in Zion — to bestow on them a crown of beauty instead of ashes, the oil of gladness instead of mourning, and a garment of praise instead of a spirit of despair. They will be called oaks of righteousness, a planting of the Lord for the display of his splendour.'*

6. **Spirit of Despair.** The 'spirit of despair' mentioned in verse 3, can stimulate us to seek the Lord. We sometimes need to reach the point of despair, when we can no longer rely on ourselves and acknowledge that we are sinners

needing a Saviour.

7. **New Covenant.** Isaiah 61:4–7 lists the wonderful benefits of being blessed by God. Verse 8 of this passage speaks of the everlasting covenant that God has made with born-again believers — a covenant in which the prophet Jeremiah wrote that God would place His law in our minds and write it in our hearts. The old covenant was written (during Moses' time) on tablets of stone but this new covenant is written in our hearts by God. It is this new covenant that we remember as we partake in the Holy Communion.

8. **Rejoicing and Loving God.** As a result of what God has done, according to Isaiah 61:10, this causes us to, *'delight greatly in the Lord and rejoice in God.'* The more a Christian appreciates what God has done and who He is, the more he wants to rejoice in Him. Christ told us that the greatest commandment is to love God with all our hearts, soul and mind. In our natural selves this love is not possible but the more we get to know and appreciate God through prayer and Bible study, the more we will become motivated by the Holy Spirit to love and praise God.

Chapter 5
The Invisible Fight for the Heart

1. *The heart is deceitful above all things and beyond cure. Who can understand it?* (Jeremiah 17:9). In this invisible fight over who controls our heart we have two problems. First, we possess a deceitful heart and second, we fight a deceitful enemy (Satan). Our deceitful heart can result in us even deceiving ourselves into believing how good we are, while our deceitful enemy subtly makes us think our problems can be sorted by our own efforts and all that is required to improve our lives is better education, developing civilization and restructuring society. In reality our problems are not solved by ourselves but rather by allowing God to deal with the fallen condition of our hearts as a result of our slavery to sin.

2. **The term 'heart' is used in scripture to describe the inner life of a person.** The Lord makes it clear why we sin — it is a matter of the heart. Our hearts have been inclined towards sin from the time we were born. Our Lord Jesus Christ said, *'For out of the heart come evil thoughts, murder, adultery, sexual immorality, theft, false testimony, slander'* (Matthew 15:19). We need a spiritual 'heart transplant,' undertaken by the Great Physician — the Lord Jesus Christ.

3. **A pure heart.** *'Create in me a pure heart, O God, and renew a steadfast spirit within me. Do not cast me from your presence or take your Holy Spirit from me. Restore to me the joy of your salvation and grant me a willing spirit, to sustain me.'* David wrote this psalm in repentance to God after committing murder and adultery. He was known as 'a man after God's own heart,' so knew the secret behind a restored life, which is the motivation that comes from a deep desire for a purified heart. *'Create in me a pure heart, O God, and renew a steadfast spirit within me'* (Psalm 51:10). Christ taught, *'Blessed are the pure in heart, for they shall see God.'*

4. **We, like David, need to understand that we are sinners.** Romans 3:23 states that, *'All have sinned and fall short of the glory of God.'* Those who don't believe in Christ need to acknowledge (under the prompting and guidance of the Holy Spirit) that they are entangled in slavery to sin, so need to deeply repent, believe in Christ and receive Him as Lord and Saviour.

5. **Philippians 1:21, *'For to me, to live is Christ and to die is gain.'*** Paul, who wrote these words, knew that there was no other way to live a full and satisfying life, apart from 'living in Christ.' To those who do not believe in Christ, life on earth is all there is, and so it is natural for them to strive for this world's values — money, popularity, power, pleasure and prestige.

6. ***'Come near to God and he will come near to you'* (James 4:8).** In one of the Christian hostels in which I was

involved in Clapham, an ex-prisoner told me that in his daily individual prayer time he always started the day by reading a psalm. He found this a good way to 'come near to God.' As Christians we need to find ways of drawing close to Christ and learn to talk to Him, developing our relationship with Him. All this is fine, provided that we have truly repented of our sins and not allowed the tentacles of habitual sin to remain in our lives. Satan is described like a crouching lion, waiting for the opportunity to attack and try to destroy our faith: he knows us well, having been successful in tempting us, particularly when we were unbelievers.

7. **Spiritual Warfare.** '*But one thing I do: forgetting what is behind and straining towards what is ahead, I press on towards the goal to win the prize for which God has called me heavenwards in Christ Jesus.*' (Philippians 3:13–14). Whenever I read these two verses, I envisage Paul leaning forward, battling against a strong, stormy wind — this is an illustration of spiritual warfare.

8. **'We need to keep a short account with God.'** By this I mean, as Christians, we need to daily check if there are any outstanding, unconfessed sins in our hearts, spoiling our fellowship with God: if there are, we must genuinely repent and turn from them. Through the ministry of the Holy Spirit and repentance, our sins are forgiven, and we are back in fellowship with God.

Chapter 6
How and why did I come into this world?

Prayer. Dear Father, we praise you that you are all-seeing, all-knowing, all-powerful, and everywhere present. We marvel that you know us and are with us and that your greatest gift is to allow us to know you: please give us the spirit of wisdom and revelation in the knowledge of Jesus Christ. Amen.

1. Introduction. Christ encourages us to, 'S*eek and you will find*' (Matthew 7:7). We need to learn to seek and find out answers to fundamental questions about life — to this end I will address two of these questions: 'How and Why did I come into this world?'

2. Many years ago, when I was working as a probation officer, I visited a prisoner who told me how, in a depressed state, while he was sitting alone in his cell, he saw an ant crawling across the concrete floor. This stimulated him to think through a series of questions: "Who made that ant?" "If God made that ant, did He make me?" "If He made me, what is His purpose for my life?"

3. **How did I come to this world?**
1) Nehemiah 9:6, '*You alone are the Lord. You made the heavens, even the highest heavens, and all their starry host, the earth and all that is in it, the seas and all that is in*

them. You give life to everything, and the multitudes of heaven worship you.' This verse states that God made the earth and all that is in it, which includes us. This truth is summarized in the first verse of the Bible (Genesis 1:1), *'In the beginning God created the heavens and the earth.'*

2) When God created us, He took an active interest in our well-being. Psalm 139:13-15, *'For you* (God) *created my inmost being; you knit me together in my mother's womb. I praise you because I am fearfully and wonderfully made; your works are wonderful, I know that full well. My frame was not hidden from you when I was made in the secret place. When I was woven together in the depths of the earth, your eyes saw my unformed body.'*

3) God sees everything: even inside our mother's womb — referred to here as, 'the secret place.' Often, when parents first see their new born child, they call the birth a miracle, which indeed it is — it's just a pity that most don't develop their thinking a little further by enquiring who performed this miracle of creating such a beautiful little life.

4) We should have as much respect for ourselves as our Maker has for us. When we feel worthless or even begin to hate ourselves, we should remember that the Holy Spirit is ready and willing to work within us.

4. **Why did I come to this world?** Having made me, what was God's purpose in bringing me into this world? I believe it is because He is desperately keen to have a personal relationship with me. We will now look at the two ways God makes Himself known to us — firstly, through His Creation and, secondly, through His Son.

5. God's Creation

1) Romans 1:20, *'For since the creation of the world God's invisible qualities — his eternal power and divine nature — have been clearly seen, being understood from what has been made, so that men are without excuse.'* To believe that the universe just happened by chance is absurd, as its design, intricacy and orderliness can only point to a wise and skilful Creator.

2) This vast world is in the hands of God. Some might ask how we can reconcile the fact that God is in control, with the existence of evil and suffering in the world. God did not create evil, but He can and does sometimes permit its presence. Nothing is out of God's control. As a result, through adversity, many Christians have learnt to persevere and overcome evil and suffering.

3) God does not expect us to face evil and suffering without having first suffered Himself. Christ died on the cross, and as a result Christians can receive grace and power to face evil and suffering, emulating Christ's example as, 'the suffering servant' (Isaiah chapter 53).

4) Why do people fail to acknowledge the existence of God when the proof of His existence and power is before their very eyes in nature? It is probably due to the stubbornness of Man's fallen, sinful nature, which the Bible says is at enmity against God.

5) If an unbeliever acknowledges the fantastic displays of God's craftsmanship, with the heavens giving dramatic evidence to God's existence, power love and care, the next logical step is for the person to start asking some basic, fundamental questions, such as, "How can I please God?" and "After I die what will happen to me?" This train of

thought should lead on to a realization of the importance of believing in Christ.

6) Psalm 19:1, '*The heavens declare the glory of God and the skies proclaim the work of His hands.*' Despite this psalmist's description of the fantastic display of God's creative genius, this in itself does not inform us about how we can have a relationship with Almighty God, which we will consider now.

6. <u>God makes Himself known to us through His Son</u>

1) Christianity is not essentially a matter of keeping a set of rules, but rather, it is about getting to know God by forming a relationship with His Son. Hebrews 1:3, '*The Son is the radiance of God's glory and the exact representation of his being.*' Christ indicated that on Judgement Day, the main criteria for eternal life will be whether or not people know Him as a personal Saviour.

2) When one buys a new appliance, it is important to follow the maker's instructions. In a similar way, the Bible sets out Our Maker's instructions. The Bible is direct and punchy about instructions. One such example is in Mark 1:14-15, '*Jesus went into Galilee, proclaiming the good news of God. "The time has come," he said. "The kingdom of God is near. Repent and believe the good news."* Christ said that two things are required of us — repentance and believing the good news, which we consider in the next two paragraphs.

3) 'Repentance' here means turning away from sin towards Christ — as we repent, God can forgive our sins due to Christ's sacrificial death. The normal result of true repentance and belief in the Lord Jesus Christ, is that the

Father forgives our sins, and we are delivered from our sinful nature. This does not mean we will never sin again but that we are no longer under a slavery to sin.

4) 'Believing the good news' refers to believing in the gospel of Christ, which results in a new relationship with the Lord Jesus Christ. This does not mean becoming a reformed person but rather, a regenerated person with a new nature provided by God. The gospel enables us to know Almighty God through His Son: one of His purposes in coming to this world was to reveal God's character to us. As our spirits are awakened by the Holy Spirit, we begin to sense the presence of God.

7. Conclusion

1) Prisoners have much time to think deeply about life. Being in custody is a real leveller: most prisoners, on entering the prison system, find it a 'shock to the system.' On the 'outside' they would probably have relied on being 'accepted' as a result of status symbols, such as 'being tough,' employment, family life, status, dignity and purpose. However, on the 'inside' most of these 'struts of life' seem to be 'kicked away,' leaving a feeling of vulnerability, sometimes resulting in a desire to seek God.

2) Many people today are content to be entertained for hours watching television, 'glued' to their mobile phones, or lose themselves in pleasure, drink and drugs. However, the wise thing to do is to follow the example of the prisoner, who as a result of watching the ant crossing his cell floor (see paragraph 2), began to consider some of the important questions in life.

3) Below I summarize the Biblical answers to the two

questions we considered: —

- How I came into this world? God made and placed me in the world: creation and Christ confirm that this world belongs to the Creator God.

— Why I came into the world? It was in order to have a relationship with God through His Son, the Lord Jesus Christ.

7. Prayer. Father, if we have not already questioned our existence and purpose in life, may the Holy Spirit lead us into earnestly seeking the answers to some of the deep questions in life. As we do this may we be drawn to the conclusion that the creative power and purpose in our physical and spiritual lives come from the Lord Jesus Christ and that through repentance and faith in Him, we might discover the joy and freedom of having a personal relationship with Him. We ask this in Jesus' name. Amen.

Chapter 7
Pentecostal Revival

1. Pentecost was the first in a series of revivals in the Christian Church. Every revival is to some extent a repetition of what happened at Pentecost.

2. During revivals members of the Church, as a result of the stimulus of the Holy Spirit, are given a certain assurance of the truth. At Pentecost, Peter received a special, spiritual ability to teach about the Lord. During revivals there is a sense of wonder and luminosity in the faces of those who encounter the Lord. Acts 2:41-43, *'Those who accepted his message were baptised, and about three thousand were added to their number that day. They devoted themselves to the apostles' teaching and to the fellowship, to the breaking of bread and to prayer. Everyone was filled with awe, and many wonders and miraculous signs were done by the apostles.'*

3. In order to obtain a sense of the attitudes and emotions of the crowds at Jerusalem on Palm Sunday, Passover and Pentecost, I have written a creative report by a fictional Egyptian Jew, based on relevant Biblical passages. In AD 30 this Jew had an extended stay in Jerusalem after the Passover Feast and this was his testimony:

1) *"I arrived on Sunday; it was an extremely hot day. Having walked from Egypt, which took several weeks, I just wanted 'to put my feet up.' Sam, my cousin, with whom I was staying, had just met me and 'squashed' my idea of an 'afternoon nap.' Instead, he suggested we see Jesus coming into Jerusalem — he had a great respect for Jesus, who had healed him from blindness. Although he was grateful for what Jesus had done in healing him, Sam was not one of Jesus' followers.*

2) *Sam thrust a palm branch into my hand and off we went to the procession. I was surprised to see how humble and in control Jesus seemed. We made a canopy with our palm branches for Him to ride under on a young donkey. I was caught up with the loud praise the crowd was giving Jesus. Someone shouted to me above the noise that Jesus was going to release us from the Romans. I was all for that, so felt quite excited.*

3) *A few days later, Sam and I went to Pilate's palace. Having recently watched Jesus' triumphant entry into Jerusalem, I was amazed to see Jesus on trial at Pilate's palace. It was annoying that a little earlier Jesus just gave Himself up to a few guards, who had been sent to arrest Him — there was no fight. A fine example of a deliverer! How could a man like that claim to be our deliverer and just give up at the first sign of trouble?*

4) *Pilate offered us the choice of freeing Jesus or Barabbas. For me and nearly all the crowd, it was no contest — it had to be Barabbas. Although he had been a bit naughty, at least it was in a good cause — murder and rebellion against the Romans is fine by me. Pilate then asked us what to do with Jesus and a huge shout rang out,*

"Crucify Him." Of course, I joined the crowd in this shout. All this seemed very odd to me: Pilate was supposed to be the judge and all he did was ask us what to do. That is the Romans for you! With leaders like Pilate, I don't know how the Romans rule the world!

5) I didn't stay for the crucifixion — don't like blood. Anyway, I needed to catch up with some sleep.

6) Sam let me stay on for a few more weeks — I didn't fancy the long walk back to Egypt in the heat. Sometime later, Sam and I were looking round the city when we heard a huge commotion. When we got closer, Sam told me not to worry as he recognized a few Christians, whom he thought had been drinking heavily, as they were grieving the loss of their leader. I wasn't so sure they had been drinking because one of them, who certainly didn't look like an Egyptian, spoke in my language — very strange!

7) A guy stood up. I was later told his name was, 'Peter.' He said that the disciples had not been drinking but were filled with the Holy Spirit. I wondered who or what was the Holy Spirit. Peter talked for quite a while and at one stage accused us of having Jesus killed by shouting for His crucifixion. The cheek of it! Then something really odd happened. I burst into tears! Don't ask me why. It was as if something inside just got hold of me.

8) I joined the crowd again, in anguish shouting with others to the disciples, "What shall we do?" Peter told us to repent and be baptised in the name of Jesus Christ for the forgiveness of sins. I sure repented and realized something had happened to me: 'my heart was strangely warmed.' I was later told that this was the work of the Holy Spirit. However, I was left wondering about the Man, whose death

I had clamoured for and started crying again: my emotions were all over the place. By this stage I was prostrate on the ground.

9) One of the disciples knelt beside me and I felt better. I had a sort of peace, when the disciple told me that Jesus had risen from the dead — Peter had said this earlier in his address to the crowd. Now it really struck home and I was beginning to believe: it's difficult to explain, but something inside urged me to believe. I began to realize that with Jesus anything was possible. The disciple told me that as I had repented, I could ask the living Lord Jesus into my life. I did this and a great weight seemed to fall off me and I felt really free for the first time. I later learned that I was one of 3,000 people who had believed in Jesus on that day.

10) The disciple told me that he would collect me the next day from my cousin's house to attend a meeting to listen to the teaching of one of the apostles. The next day it was Peter again doing the teaching — they don't give the man a break! Peter told us that he believed God had forgiven us for being double-minded, in that our initial reaction to Jesus was to have Him crucified. He said that after our baptism in a couple of days' time, we would be in danger of arrest from the authorities, but that the Lord Jesus, through the Holy Spirit, would be our guide and comforter.

11) Peter reminded us that our ancestors in the wilderness had been bitten by snakes after complaining to God (Numbers 21:4-9). Having checked out with God, Moses had been told to place a brass serpent on a pole in the sight of all the people so that everyone who was bitten and looked on the serpent would live. Peter said that Jesus had referred to this incident, when He said (John 3:14–15),

'Just as Moses lifted up the snake in the desert, so the Son of Man must be lifted up, that everyone who believes in him may have eternal life.' Peter then encouraged us to spend the rest of our lives with our eyes fixed on Jesus, 'the author and perfecter of our faith' (Hebrews 12:2).

12)Peter told us not to just drift in our lives but to show forth the fruit (spiritual sort) of the Spirit. One of the fruits he emphasised was self-discipline, which would enable and encourage us to gaze upon Jesus and be led by the Holy Spirit. I know it is going to be a difficult life as a Christian but I no longer feel alone, as I am aware of Jesus' presence. I now love praising Him, especially when reading the Psalms."

4. This fictional autobiography covers the time of Pentecost when the New Testament Church experienced the first revival. The many subsequent revivals have often mirrored some of the spiritual phenomena and teaching at Pentecost. A recent major revival in the UK was the 1904 Welsh Revival, when not only did 50,000 people become Christians but whole communities changed, with some courts, prisons and pubs closing, due to a lack of clients. The most common feature about revivals is that they occur when the spiritual life of a nation is at a low ebb, as currently is the case in much of Europe. Following is some information about revivals:

1) They are glorious periods of re-awakening that have often followed periods of great spiritual drought, deadness, apathy and lifelessness in the Church. There have been revivals in the past in many parts of the world, including Africa, China, Manchuria, Korea and India.

2) In 1859 a revival began in the USA, spread to Northern Ireland, Wales in 1904 and then on to parts of Scotland and England.

3) The revival in UK prior to that was in 1759, an evangelical awakening during the time of Whitfield and the two Wesley brothers, when the churches were so filled with life and power that the whole society was beneficially affected.

4) In January 1994 there was what might be termed a 'mini-revival', called 'The Toronto Blessing,' which began in the Toronto Airport Vineyard Church, in Canada. A number of Christians from different countries visited the Airport Vineyard and returned with this blessing, passing it on to their own churches.

5) Several churches in the UK were beneficially affected, including Holy Trinity Church in Brompton and the twenty-two UK Vineyard Churches. At the time I attended Whitton Vineyard Church in South West London. It was an exciting time seeing the power of the Holy Spirit being manifested. Sometimes the school, where we worshipped, looked as if it had been struck by an explosion, with many prostrate on the floor, while others knelt beside them praying.

6) This blessing did not last long, nor did it have a particularly strong influence on the people 'outside the Church.' In revivals the usual pattern is for the Holy Spirit to fall on a church meeting, with such a massive, life-changing effect that the newly emboldened Christians become effective in evangelizing unbelievers in their neighbourhood.

7) It would seem that 'The Toronto Blessing' was not

always handled appropriately by some of the Christian leaders, who were involved with this movement of the Spirit.

5. Following are some points made by Dr Martyn Lloyd-Jones in his book, 'Revival,' in respect to the UK over the last two centuries. He says that there are three similar features in revivals:

1) <u>God used very ordinary men to start the revivals.</u> John Wesley was a complete failure in his ministry until 24th May 1738, when he completely changed, as a result of being filled with power through the Holy Spirit. In 1859 another ordinary minister, called David Morgan, started the Northern Ireland revival. In the 1904 Welsh Revival Evan Roberts was a very ordinary man, whom God empowered for that revival. These experiences reflect the experiences of the weak helpless disciples, who were totally changed from being scared and disloyal to the Lord at the time of His arrest, to humble, courageous followers, having been filled with the blazing power and fire of the Holy Spirit at Pentecost.

2) <u>Revivals often start in 'out of the way' places.</u> The Northern Ireland Revival started in a small village, called Connor, while the 1904 Welsh Revival started in a little hamlet, called Trevecca. God quite often chooses insignificant places to display His will and power — for instance, He chose insignificant Bethlehem, as His Son's birthplace.

3) <u>A revival usually leads unbelievers to exclaiming, 'What is this?'</u> This was the response of the townspeople of Jerusalem on the day of Pentecost. Dr Martyn Lloyd-Jones

writes, '*revival.... is something that comes like a flood. Astounding things happen, and of such a magnitude that men are left amazed, astonished[2].*'

6. Dr Martyn Lloyd-Jones studied revivals in some depth, so his conclusions are authoritative, therefore as 'ordinary people' we should be encouraged to pray for revival, particularly in the wake of Covid-19.

7. <u>Prayer.</u> Father, we have heard of your fame in bringing about revivals according to your perfect plan and will. We know that when You act in power many come to faith in Your Son, through the ministry of the Holy Spirit. While our land deserves your judgement, in Your grace, please remember mercy and bring us revival, in Jesus Name, Amen.

---

[2] Most of paragraph 5 taken from Martyn Lloyd-Jones, *Revival*, Crossway Books, Wheaton, Illinois, 1992.

Chapter 8
Philippians and Prisoners

1. We are going to consider two important aspects of Christ's life from Philippians 2:1–12 — Christ's humility and crucifixion. Paul was in prison when he wrote this letter. No doubt the influence of his custodial circumstances effected his letter writing. Whilst in prison Paul used his time constructively, writing this letter of joy and encouragement to the Philippians. During his two-year period in custody, he also wrote letters to the Ephesians, Colossians and Philemon.

2. **Christ's Humility** Philippians 2:3 records Paul's words, '*Do nothing out of selfish ambition or vain conceit, but in humility consider others better than yourselves.*' Paul was encouraging Christian unity, rather than selfishness, amongst the Philippians. In the subsequent verses he reminds them that although Christ was equal with God, He became a servant and humbled Himself, even dying for us.

1) Paul said that our attitude should be the same as that of Christ in regard to humility. Being humble involves having a right perspective about ourselves. It does not mean that we should put ourselves down, but rather that we should understand our true condition before God — we are sinners, saved by God's grace.

2) James 4:6, '*God opposes the proud, but gives grace*

to the humble.' Pride is the opposite of humility. If we are proud, God is automatically against us, and while in this state He cannot forgive us.

3) Many unbelievers show what Paul describes as, 'selfish ambition or vain conceit'. Some describe themselves as 'leading a good life,' but it all depends on what a person's criteria is for leading a good life. In Christ's view the greatest command, and therefore the main criteria for acceptance is 'to love God with all one's heart, soul and mind.'

4) In regard to humility, to some extent prisoners are in an advantageous position compared to those not in prison. The criminal justice system labels prisoners as 'offenders', which enables them more easily to acknowledge that before God they are sinners, who have in most cases offended against God's laws.

5) An example of humility I saw in Jonathan Aitken. He had all the trappings of this carnal world, being a promising cabinet minister and wealthy and well respected in the Tory party. He lost most of these carnal trappings as a result of his imprisonment. I once asked if he was pleased that he had gone to prison. He told me that he was pleased, as it was in prison that his faith was ignited by Christ. I could see in Jonathan that nothing in this world could compare to the pure joy of a personal relationship with the Lord Jesus. Jonathan is currently a prison chaplain.

3. **Christ's Crucifixion.** Philippians 2:8, '*And* (Christ) *being found in appearance as a man, he humbled himself and became obedient to death — even death on a cross!'* One might wonder whether there was some other way for

Man to be reconciled to God, instead of Christ having to die on a cross? Perhaps God could have just made a declaration from heaven stating that He had decided to forgive Man of all sin. Although much easier, God could not do this, as it would mean that He was no longer a righteous, just judge, but instead acting like an overindulgent parent, by just letting us off the punishment of death for our sins, which He had previously declared.

4. The Trinity had given thought to this tricky issue before the creation of the world and decided that there was only one way to solve the problem of wayward humanity. They decided that as Adam, Mankind's representative, had disobeyed God, a man had to secure reconciliation between God and Man. In voluntarily becoming Man, Christ did not give up His deity but temporarily set aside some of His glory and power: in doing this He did not cease to be God. During His earthly ministry, Christ was both fully God and fully Man.

5. Paul made good use of His time in prison, especially in his letter writing, by encouraging members of new churches that he had been involved in setting up. He also sought to evangelize his jailors. He was fixated by the Gospel of Christ and had an infectious, vivacious faith. He sometimes 'exploded' with amazing spiritual concepts and insightful knowledge about God, which probably originated from his meeting the Risen Lord on the Damascus Road, as well as his experiences in the 'third heaven.' Joy and humility were characteristics which shone through Paul's life:

1) Joy was Paul's hallmark and should also be the hallmark of all Christians.

2) His joy was in the Lord, who has a special affinity with those on the margins of society, like prisoners, especially those who recognize their need for a Saviour.

3) The humility that Paul wrote about was epitomized in Christ's entry into paradise — instead of taking one of His beloved Apostles, He entered heaven, accompanied by an unknown ex-offender, with whom He had only spoken a few words. The key was that this particular ex-offender had what Paul wrote about (recorded in Philippians 2:5), '*Your attitude should be the same as that of Christ Jesus.*' The offender went into paradise with an attitude of humility and brokenness, acknowledging his sin and recognizing Jesus as Lord. We should show the same attitude.

Chapter 9
Judgement Day

1. Judgements in the legal system in the UK are based on 'precedent law,' which involves 'following a precedent or rule established in a previous legal case that is binding or persuasive for the court deciding subsequent cases with similar facts.' Our present court sentences have been developed over centuries of past court rulings and judgements.

2. The Lord Judge Jesus Christ on Judgement Day will also follow God the Father's precedent law, including the Ten Commandments and the Lord's summary of these in first loving God and also our neighbours as ourselves. God has made it clear what criteria He will use when making judgements, so that we have no excuse if we fail to live up to His high expectations of us.

3. When we are judged as Christians, it may feel strange because Our Judge is also living within us, '*Christ in you, the hope of glory*' (Colossians 1:27).

4. There will be quite a 'build up' to Judgement Day with plenty of signs preceding and heralding this momentous event. In Matthew 24:29–30 Jesus described the signs as follows, "*the sun will be darkened, and the*

moon will not give its light; the stars will fall from the sky, and the heavenly bodies will be shaken. At that time the sign of the Son of Man will appear in the sky, and all the nations of the earth will mourn." Why will the nations mourn? It is because unbelievers will suddenly realize that they have chosen the wrong side.

5. Jesus will send out his angels with a loud trumpet call to gather His elect throughout the universe. Presumably, after that He will commence His judgement. In 2 Corinthians 5:10 Paul states, *'For we must all appear before the judgement seat of Christ, that each may receive what is due to him for the things done while in the body, whether good or bad.'* Everyone will be judged, irrespective of whether or not they are Christians.

6. At Judgement Day all of us must give an account of how we have lived. Our Lord explained two vital requirements for entry into the Kingdom of Heaven. **The first requirement is the acceptable quality of our personal relationship with the Lord.** Matthew 7:21–23, *'Not everyone who says to me, 'Lord, Lord,' will enter the kingdom of heaven, but only he who does the will of my Father in heaven. Many will say to me on that day, 'Lord. Lord, did we not prophesy in your name, and in your name drive out demons and perform many miracles?' Then I will tell them plainly, 'I never knew you. Away from me, you evildoers!'*

7. Jesus exposed those people who sounded religious but had no personal relationship with Him. On Judgement

Day the main criteria on which we will be judged will be the quality of our relationship with Jesus — our acceptance of Him as Saviour and our obedience to Him. It would appear from the response and language used by the people the Lord was criticizing had some familiarity with Christianity, as they used Christian terminology in their appeal for leniency to Judge Jesus.

8. **The second entry requirement for the Kingdom of Heaven concerns the way we act towards others**, which is explained by Jesus in Matthew 25:31–46. God will separate His obedient followers from pretenders and unbelievers. The evidence of our faith is manifested in our attitude and actions towards others, especially those in difficulties. What we do for others demonstrates obedience to Our Lord's instructions, to feed the hungry, give the homeless a place to stay and to look after the sick.

9. *'Do not merely listen to the word, and so deceive yourselves. Do what it says.'* (James 1:22). While we cannot earn salvation by serving and obeying God, nevertheless such actions reveal the depth and sincerity of our faith — deeds are a verification of our faith.

10. Some unbelievers claim that there is nothing after death, however this is not the view of Our Lord, who is recorded as saying in John 3:18, *'Whoever believes in him is not condemned, but whoever does not believe stands condemned already because he has not believed in the name of God's one and only Son.'* All of us will be in eternity, however it will be up to the Lord as to whether we spend

eternity in heaven or hell.

11. Man boasts of being intelligent but in spiritual matters often acts like a fool. The Bible says that *'The fool says in his heart, "There is no god"'* (Psalm 14:1). It is strange that Man seems oblivious to God's creative ingenuity, preferring to dwell on make-believe. Man's attitude seems to confirm the truth of the Biblical statement, *'The god of this age has blinded the minds of unbelievers'* (2 Corinthians 4:4).

12. Paul explains what will happen to us after death in 1 Corinthians 15:35–39, ' *"How are the dead raised? With what kind of body will they come?" How foolish! What you sow does not come to life unless it dies. When you sow, you do not plant the body that will be, but just a seed, perhaps of wheat or of something else. But God gives it a body as he has determined, and to each kind of seed he gives its own body. All flesh is not the same: Men have one kind of flesh, animals have another, birds another and fish another.'*

13. Paul compares the resurrection of our bodies with growth in the garden. Seeds placed in the ground don't grow unless they 'die' first. The plant that grows looks quite different from the seed because God gives it a new 'body'. There are different kinds of bodies — people, animals, fish and birds. Even the angels in heaven have bodies that are different in beauty and glory. Our resurrected bodies will have major differences from our earthly bodies[3].

---

[3] Paragraphs 13 and 14 taken from notes on 1 Corinthians 15:35-45 of *Life Application Bible (New Internal Version)*, Kingsway Publications,

14. Our present bodies are perishable and prone to decay, whilst our resurrected bodies will be transformed. These spiritual bodies will not be limited by the laws of nature. This does not necessarily mean we will be 'super' people, but our bodies will be different from, and more capable than, our present earthly bodies. Our spiritual bodies will not be weak, will never get sick and never die.

15. I am sure we would all prefer heaven to hell, 'clothed' in our wonderful new bodies and dwelling in the presence of our loving King. Consequently, we must remember the two main requirements for entering the Kingdom of heaven — our personal relationship with Jesus and how in His name we treat others, particularly vulnerable people in difficulties.

Eastbourne, 1988.

Chapter 10
Prayer, Worry and Anxiety

1. The effect of the Corona Virus on many has been to create worry and anxiety, as it has highlighted an awareness of the fragility of life. We will consider, firstly, the Biblical approach as to why we sometimes worry and get anxious and secondly, how Christians should respond to anxiety.

Why Some Christians Worry and are Anxious

2. The Devil was around prior to the creation of the world. Having been thrown down to the Earth, he attacked God's treasured creation, Man. Paul wrote (Ephesians 6:11–12), '… *take your stand against the devil's schemes. For our struggle is not against flesh and blood, but against the rulers, against the authorities, against the powers of this dark world and the forces of evil in the heavenly realms.*'

3. Since we are in a spiritual struggle against a powerful enemy, it is wise to adopt one of the key principles of modern warfare, which is to, 'know your enemy.' We need to recognize the hand of the Devil behind many of our anxieties. He can attack us through our minds. Most Christians have experienced thoughts, which may be evil, wrong or worrying, which are implanted in us by the Devil, as one of his tactics to tempt us to sin and worry, resulting in us becoming less fruitful in our service to God. The thoughts themselves are neither our own nor sinful — we

only sin if we accept and cherish these thoughts.

How Christians should respond to Anxiety

4. While an unbeliever is controlled by the things of the world, a Christian should be in control of himself under the Lord's guidance, being balanced and demonstrating a sense of proportion. Our Lord taught about the negative effect of anxiety. Mary, and her sister, Martha, lived in a small village, called Bethany, near Jerusalem. On one occasion, when Jesus visited them, Mary listened intently to Jesus, while Martha was busy with household chores, so the latter asked Jesus to tell Mary to assist her.

5. Jesus responded with an insightful reply (Luke 10:41), *"'Martha, Martha,"* the Lord answered, *"you are worried and upset about many things, but only one thing is needed. Mary has chosen what is better, and it will not be taken away from her.'"* Jesus told Martha that she had the wrong priorities. He was not decrying the importance of carrying out daily duties and hospitality but rather encouraging Martha to recognize the importance of taking the limited opportunity of being in His Presence and learning from Him.

6. Fear of the future is a natural extension of anxiety — this is another strategy promoted by the Devil. Fear of the future reveals unbelief: it is a complete waste of time as we do not know what will happen in the future. Worry about the future makes us paralysed in the present. In the Sermon on the Mount, Our Lord said, *'Therefore I tell you, do not worry about your life...'* (Matthew 6:25). Jesus finished His statement on this theme with these words (verse 34),

'*Therefore do not worry about tomorrow, for tomorrow will worry about itself. Each day has enough trouble of its own.*' By worrying we are disobeying God's command not to worry, revealing a lack of faith in God's wonderful provisions for us.

7. One of the nine fruits of the Spirit is self-control, which is required when tackling worrying thoughts. We should speak strongly to ourselves, exerting our influence to rid ourselves of these thoughts, recognizing that they are from the Devil. James 4:7, '*Submit yourselves, then, to God. Resist the devil, and he will flee from you.*' Self-control is involved when resisting the Devil. Paul suggests a similar strategy by adopting prayer in place of worry — (Philippians 4:6), '*Do not be anxious about anything, but in everything, by prayer and petition, with thanksgiving, present your requests to God.*' Paul suggests that the antidote to worry is prayer.

8. Some Christians offer the 'prayer of faith' for healing and become despondent when the person prayed for fails to recover. It can be in such cases that the Devil fills our minds with subtle misinformation, which can demoralize faithful Christians. For instance, on the issue of healing, the Devil might plant a question in people's minds that God is being unfair and untrue to His loving nature when refusing to grant a reasonable request from His people to heal someone. One of the Devil's successful strategies is the crafty and deceitful way he frames questions in order to cause confusion and uncertainty. He did this when tempting Adam and Eve to question the sovereignty of God.

9. Why people are not always healed, after Christians believe they have offered what they consider 'a prayer of faith,' is a question that can puzzle Christians. Here is an attempt to answer this question by seeking to understand God's perspective on prayer for healing and guidance. If God always answered prayer for healing (and guidance) with automatic healing (and automatic guidance), we would just become mechanical and this is not the way that God wants to develop His people. The term, 'prayer of faith' comes from James 5:14–15, '*Is any of you sick? He should call the elders of the church to pray over him and anoint him with oil in the name of the Lord. And the <u>prayer offered in faith</u> will make the sick person well; the Lord will raise him up.*'

10. People should only claim they are 'praying in faith,' if the Holy Spirt provides the necessary faith: this is a strong inner sense that healing will result because the Holy Spirit has implanted this faith into those praying. Whenever it is recorded in the Bible that the apostles (in the New Testament Church) prayed for healing — it happened. No doubt their extensive experience with the Lord enabled them to become attuned to the healing ministry of the Holy Spirit.

Chapter 11
A New and Living Way

'Therefore, brothers, since we have confidence to enter the Most Holy Place by the blood of Jesus, by a new and living way opened for us through the curtain, that is, his body, and since we have a great priest over the house of God, let us draw near to God with a sincere heart in full assurance of faith, having our hearts sprinkled to cleanse us from a guilty conscience and having our bodies washed with pure water' (Hebrews 10:19–22).

1. The author of Hebrews is not known. The letter was written between AD 55 and AD 70 to all Christians, but especially to the Jewish Christians, some of whom were considering leaving the Christian faith for two reasons. Firstly, they found the Christian message difficult to accept, as they were entrenched in thinking and worshipping in their traditional Jewish ways. Secondly, the Christian Church was being heavily persecuted by the cruel Roman Emperor Nero, so consequently the Jewish Christians were tempted to avoid persecution by returning to Judaism, which in the Roman Empire at that time was still legal, although Christianity was not.

2. Hebrews 10:19. *'Therefore, brothers, since we have confidence to enter the Most Holy Place by the blood of Jesus.'* Earlier in this letter the writer had acknowledged

that the former faith of these Jews (Judaism) and their new faith (Christianity) were both religions revealed by God but that Christianity was superior as it had a better covenant, or agreement, with God and a more sufficient sacrifice for sins in Christ Jesus' sacrifice of Himself on the Cross.

3. God originally made us in His image so that He could have fellowship with us. Sadly, due to Man's fall in Adam, we were excluded from God's holy presence because of our sins. The passage we are studying is part of God's great plan to reconcile us back to Himself — hence we can come into His Presence, called here, 'the Most Holy Place.' God wants to have a personal relationship with us, with our spirit mingling with His Spirit. We have been made in God's image and therefore have the capacity to know Him. The moment the Spirit quickens us with new life, our whole being senses its kinship to God and leaps up in joyous recognition of Him.

4. Hebrews 10:20. '...*By a new and living way opened for us through the curtain, that is, his body.*' In the Old Testament the Most Holy Place in the temple was sealed from view by a curtain. Only a priest could enter this holy room just once a year to offer a sacrifice for the nation's sins. But Jesus' death opened the curtain, so that all believers could spiritually come into God's presence at any time. This is 'the new and living way' opened by Christ, who died to bring us forgiveness of sins.

5. Hebrews 10:21–22. *'And since we have a great priest over the house of God, let us draw near to God with*

a sincere heart in full assurance of faith, having our hearts sprinkled to cleanse us from a guilty conscience and having our bodies washed with pure water.' In regards to having a guilty conscience, while we can fairly easily justify our actions to others, it is a different matter, seeking to justify ourselves before an all-knowing and all-seeing God, who is not fooled by our excuses. In this passage we are encouraged to draw near to God with a sincere heart.

6. How does all this work out in practice? Hebrews 10:19-22 is about how to come into God's presence, but once in His presence how do we communicate with God? If you find difficulty in coming to God in prayer, fellowship and praise, here are <u>ten practical suggestions, which I have found helpful in my prayer life</u> and you might also. The first three suggestions should come early in the prayer time:

1) **Keep a short account of sin** by frequently confessing our sins to God. The Bible states that if we regard wrongdoing in our hearts, the Lord will not hear us. This means that in our prayer times and Christian meetings, we need to check that we are not coming with unconfessed sin, otherwise this could become a spiritual blockage to the meeting.

2) **Start in the Bible.** When first coming to pray, I sense God's presence more quickly by going straight to the Bible rather than just letting my thoughts roam around, wondering about what to pray. Our initial thoughts are likely to be earthly, while the Bible brings us straight into 'heavenly thinking.' As we read, periodically stop, pray, meditate, thank and praise God, as the Spirit leads. Use the Bible passage as a springboard from which to 'dive' into

deeper communication with the Lord.

3) **When approaching God begin in praise**. Most of the prayers recorded in the Bible start by glorifying God. Imagine looking in faith at God through a microscope: as His image and personality are gradually magnified, so our hearts are progressively drawn into praising Him.

4) When considering about whom or what to pray about, try to **steer thoughts away from our own needs**. First, we need to think about the Lord, then others, and lastly, ourselves.

5) Hebrews 10:19 encourages us to **come to God in confidence**. Whilst we need to be confident when coming to God, never become overconfident, thus losing respect for our reverent, holy, eternal God. Remember, God is not our lackey, waiting for us to tell Him what to do. Show respect by listening and trying to discern His will.

6) The Lord always wants us to **retain a sincere heart** — as we have already read in Hebrews 10:22. In the Bible King David was known as a 'man after God's own heart.' Although he occasionally sinned badly, once aware of his sin, he was quick to admit it. The lesson here is that it is futile trying to hide our sin before an all-knowing God.

7) Every day try to **learn a helpful Bible verse** and think of this during the day. When in prayer, if you suddenly think of a particular verse follow it up as this sudden stimulus may have come from the Spirit of God. Psalm 23:3 states, '*He* (the Lord) *guides me in paths of righteousness.*' One way the Lord can guide us is by reminding us of appropriate verses: however, this can normally only occur if we have already learnt the relevant verses.

8) When praying in the evening one way of tuning to

69

God is by thinking through the things that have happened during the day (similar to **watching a video of your day**): as you do this, ask God for guidance about how He wants you to pray concerning these events.

9) When suddenly faced with an unexpected situation **use a 'dart' prayer**, which is a quick, brief appeal for guidance to God. Afterwards always thank God for His guidance.

10)If someone asks you to pray for them, before praying, **ask God for guidance and spiritual insight** in order to pray in line with God's will for the person concerned.

7. Prayer. Thank you, Father, that You have made us in Your image and likeness and that through the reconciling work of Your Son we can have fellowship with You. Please guide us in prayer and give us confidence to develop our relationship with you through the work of the Holy Spirit. We ask this in Jesus' Name. Amen.

Chapter 12
Our Light and Momentary Trials

Prayer. Father, we ask that through the Holy Spirit, you will enable us to set our minds on things above, not on earthly things, that we might put heaven's eternal priorities into daily practice, in Jesus' Name. Amen.

1. '*Therefore, we do not lose heart. Though outwardly we are wasting away, yet inwardly we are being renewed day by day. For our light and momentary troubles are achieving for us an eternal glory that far outweighs them all. So we fix our eyes not on what is seen, but on what is unseen. For what is seen is temporary, but what is unseen is eternal*' (2 Corinthians 4:16–18).

2. The above passage comes from Paul's letter to the weak Corinthian Church, which was surrounded by idolatry and immorality: its members struggled with their Christian faith and lifestyle. Through personal visits and letters, Paul tried to instruct them in their faith and resolve their conflicts and problems.

3. Verse 16 — '*Therefore we do not lose heart.*' Most of us 'lose heart' occasionally. This might be due to a 'knock back' on parole, a harsh letter from a family member or illness. When this happens what do we do about it? I suggest we should follow the great apostle Paul's example.

Rather than despairing, or relying on his own abilities, he concentrated on experiencing the inner strength from the Holy Spirit. He didn't let tiredness, pain or criticism force him to give up.

4. Verse 16, second half — *'Though outwardly we are wasting away, yet inwardly we are being renewed day by day.'* At the age of seventy-seven, I know what it is like to be 'wasting away' and progressively decaying. Although I try to keep fit, I realize that the older one gets the harder it is to do physical exercise, with injuries taking longer to heal. Although outwardly we are wasting away, our inner self is being renewed day after day.

5. Verse 17 — *'For our light and momentary troubles are achieving for us an eternal glory that far outweighs them all.'* How can our troubles achieve eternal glory? We should not allow our troubles to diminish our faith or disillusion us. Instead, we should realize that there is purpose in suffering, so that we can better identify with Our Lord's suffering. While God is concerned when we are in pain, He also knows that it is while in pain or difficulties that we tend to appeal to Him for help: it is as if pain is a megaphone through which God speaks.

6. Young children tend to seek 'instant gratification' — some adults do the same thing! However, God is often looking at our long term good, which may be to teach us patience and perseverance. He is preparing us for both this life and the next. Paul is advocating that our troubles are 'momentary' and 'short-lived' compared to the eternal glory

in heaven in Christ's Presence. This does not mean us 'putting on a brave face' but rather, seeking God's inner peace through the belief that God is in control and will watch over us, whatever happens.

7. Have you considered what 'eternity' would be like? Christians not only have a personal relationship with Christ on this Earth but will also live with Him forever in the next. The well-known evangelist, Billy Graham, shortly before his death, told some friends not to worry about him as he was just going to move his address to heaven!

8. Verse 18 — *'So we fix our eyes not on what is seen but what is unseen. For what is seen is temporary, but what is unseen is eternal.'* Science is popular and influential in our day and age and largely based on what is seen. It is defined as, 'the study of nature and behaviour of the physical universe, based on observation, experiment and measurement.' Most people fix their understanding on what can be scientifically proved. Scientists mould the views of our current society. Consequently, the unseen spiritual world can be a difficult concept for many people.

9. Christians learn to view the world from both a physical and spiritual perspective and most would perceive humans as being composed of the following three different elements — soul, body, and spirit. Our soul is described in the Oxford Dictionary as, 'the moral, emotional or intellectual nature of a person.' The soul and body mainly relate to people and things on earth, while God also gives us a spirit to enable us to relate to Him, especially through

the Holy Spirit. Unbelievers are not so conscious of God because their spirits are dormant and unresponsive to God. When 'born again,' using Christ's words, we become responsive to God through our regenerated spirits.

10. Why have we been given a spirit which we cannot see? We have been given a spirit so that we can communicate with God, through our spirit. He is a loving God, who made us in His likeness in order that we might have fellowship with Him. Whether or not we are a Christian, we all have a spirit but in unbelievers the spirit is in a deep sleep. Christ said we must be 'born again.' By this He was talking about a spiritual rebirth, which gives eternal life to the unconscious spirit in an unbeliever.

Chapter 13
Christ in you, the Hope of Glory

1. *'Christ in you, the hope of glory,'* (Colossians 1:27) is a phrase in a letter that Paul wrote while in prison to the church in Colosse. He never visited this church, which had developed some errors of faith, so his main purpose in writing was to rectify these errors by teaching the centrality of Christ. Colossians 1:27 is God's glorious mystery, which is at the heart of the Christian gospel, revealing the nature of our relationship with Christ. We are going to look at the two halves (in bold type below) of this phrase.

2. **"Christ in you."** We need to consider several aspects of this spiritual union between Christ and ourselves:

1) *'The man without the Spirit does not accept the things that come from the Spirit of God, for they are foolishness to him, and he cannot understand them, because they are spiritually discerned.'* (1 Corinthians 2:14). Prior to spiritual new birth, we probably found the idea of making a relationship with God foolish. However, with a regenerated spirit, we gradually become attuned to spiritual matters. Like a tone-deaf person who suddenly begins to appreciate music, it becomes a new and exciting experience.

2) After we are 'born again' we begin to discover the joy of abiding in Christ Jesus. We sense the thrill and

wonder of being in the presence of God. We might want to stay in His presence for hours, being reluctant to leave. Prisoners have plenty of time to do this, although it can be difficult when sharing a cell with an unbeliever.

3) This relationship with Christ is difficult to describe but is available to those with 'spiritual receptivity,' as explained by a Christian author, A.W. Tozer, who writes, '*I venture to suggest that one vital quality which well-known men of God, like Moses, Isaiah, David and Paul had, was spiritual receptivity. Something in them was open to heaven, something which urged them Godward. Without attempting anything like a profound analysis, I shall say simply that they had a spiritual awareness and that they went on to cultivate it until it became the biggest thing in their lives. They differed from the average person in that when they felt the inward longing, they did something about it. They acquired the lifelong habit of spiritual response. Christ is trying to get our attention, to reveal Himself to us, to communicate with us[4].*'

4) To stimulate this 'spiritual receptivity' we need to experience 'Christ in us' to enable us to love God and our neighbour. Love does not come easily: it is not a case of trying to work up the emotion of love. Love comes from God and energizes our faith. What differentiates the Christian life from other religions is that Christ requires us to love our enemies. There is an element of discipline about love. John 14:21 records Christ's words, '*Whoever has my commands and obeys them, he is the one who loves me. He who loves me will be loved by my Father, and I will love him*

---

[4] A. W. Tozer, *The Pursuit of God,'* Christian Publications, Camp Hill, Pennsylvania, 1993.

and show myself to him.' Christ wants us to show our love by keeping His commandments.

3. Let us now consider the last part of the phrase that we are studying in its scriptural context. *'The mystery that has been kept hidden for ages and generations but is now disclosed to the saints. To them God has chosen to make known among the Gentiles the glorious riches of this mystery, which is Christ in you,* **the hope of glory.'** (Colossians 1:26–27)

4. In Paul's epistle to the Colossians he was seeking to address some of the errors in the Colossian Church, one of which was false teachers, who believed that spiritual perfection was a secret and hidden plan that only a few privileged people could discover. The secret plan was meant to be exclusive. Paul said that he was proclaiming the word of God in its fullness, not just part of the plan. He also called God's plan a 'mystery that has been kept hidden for ages and generations' not in the sense that only a few would understand, but because it was hidden until Christ came[5]. Through Christ it was made open to all. God's secret plan is 'Christ in you, the hope of glory' — God planned to have his Son, Jesus Christ, live in the hearts of all who believe in Him — even Gentiles, like the Colossians.

5. The Christians in Paul's day were being severely persecuted, with most of the apostles becoming martyrs. Therefore, Paul sought to encourage Christians with the

---

[5] Taken from notes on Colossians 1:26, 27 from *Life Application Bible (New Internal Version)*, Kingsway Publications, Eastbourne, 1988.

hope and expectation of the glory that would come to those in Christ Jesus. Through the death and resurrection of Jesus Christ, believers will finally be glorified in heaven. All human glory derives from God.

Chapter 14
Why Covid?

1. God is the Creator of our universe and is in complete control of this world, so there is no way that the Covid pandemic could have been introduced into our world without the foreknowledge and approval of God. Either He gave the Devil permission for this pandemic, or God sent the pandemic for His own purpose. This article will consider these two possibilities.

2. The first possibility is that **God gave permission to the Devil for the outbreak of Covid.** There is a precedent for the Devil being given permission to tempt someone: the Devil asked to tempt Job and the Lord replied, *"Very well, then, everything he has is in your hands, but on the man himself do not lay a finger."* (Job 1:12).

3. We are all currently engaged in a spiritual battle but in this scientific age we find it hard to conceptualize this. In Ephesians 6:12 Paul describes this struggle as being, *'not against flesh and blood, but against the rulers, against the authorities, against the powers of this dark world and against spiritual forces of evil in the heavenly realms.'*

4. In order to be prepared to fight this battle we need to understand and utilize one of the key principles of

modern warfare, which is 'to know your enemy.' This entails acquiring a good understanding of the Devil, including his aim, strategy, tactics, armaments and strength.

5. In order to understand the Devil, we need to start by considering pre-cosmic time — that being before the world was created. The Biblical teaching is that from the beginning God created the hosts of heaven (mainly composed of angels) for His own ends. They ministered to Him and were given freedom of choice. One of them, known as Lucifer, or the Devil, became 'big-headed' and had grandiose ideas about being like God.

6. God could not tolerate the Devil in heaven. What happened next is described in Revelations 12:7, '*And there was war in heaven. Michael and his angels fought against the dragon*' (the Devil), who was not strong enough and the Devil and a third of the heavenly host, who were on his side, were '*hurled to the earth.*' (Revelation 12:13). Hence the Devil was around on Earth prior to the creation of human beings, who became the Devil's prime target, being made in God's image and precious to God.

7. The Devil's strategy and tactics are acknowledged in the Bible as being fairly effective. (2 Corinthians 4:4) '*The god of this age* (the *Devil*) *has blinded the minds of unbelievers, so that they cannot see the light of the gospel of the glory of Christ.*' Satan's work is to deceive: the allure of money, power and pleasure blinds people from seeing the light of Christ's gospel. John 8:44 records Christ's description of the Devil as, '*a murderer from the beginning,*

not holding the truth, for there is no truth in him:' currently Covid suits the latter's murderous intentions.

8. There is no truth in the Devil because he is a deceiver. The Bible indicates that he brings about anxiety, fear and mental illness, all of which are currently increasing during this Covid crisis. Nevertheless, our conquering hero, the Lord Jesus Christ, through His death on the Cross, has secured the Devil's ultimate defeat to be carried out at a time to be decided by God. This substantiates 1 John 3:8, *'The reason the Son of God appeared was to destroy the devil's work.'*

9. The second possible reason for the Covid outbreak is that **God sent it for His own purpose.** In the Old Testament there are several incidents when God sent judgement on those with 'hardened hearts,' who had had rejected Him. One such incident is recorded in Exodus 32:35, when the Lord struck the people with a plague, because they had made a golden calf idol, whilst Moses was receiving the Ten Commandments direct from God.

10. God's judgements upon our sins reveal His love, mercy and justice in desiring to reconcile us back to Himself. The prophet Isaiah makes a relevant and interesting point: (Isaiah 26:9), *'When your* (God's) *judgements come upon the earth, the people of the world learn righteousness.'* This statement reveals God's purpose in sending judgements on the earth, which is to chasten people so that they might respond positively to His wake-up call by learning righteousness. Christ spoke about

righteousness: He told His disciples that after His Ascension the Holy Spirit would convict them of righteousness, enabling them to live in a right relationship with God.

11. God uses adversity to train and hone us to become more like Christ. Rather than complain about our troubled circumstances as a result of Covid, we need to emulate the attitude of James, who believed that during trials we should show a positive attitude because of what the experience of trials can produce in our lives. James 1:2–4, '*Consider it pure joy, my brothers, whenever you face trials of many kinds, because you know that the testing of your faith develops perseverance. Perseverance must finish its work so that you may be mature and complete, not lacking anything.*' Psalm 119:71 reinforces this positive outlook during suffering, '*It was good for me to be afflicted so that I might learn your decrees.*'

12. Covid has exposed the fragility of life, so challenging unbelievers to ask profound questions about life and death (normally a taboo discussion subject in our country). High unemployment means that many have had more time to consider some of the deep questions in life. This searching for God in a spirit of humility appears to be fostered by a fear of Covid. An indication of this searching is the increased interest and involvement in church services, via the internet. God is working His purposes out but not always in the way we might expect.

13. God's wrath reveals His loving, compassionate

heart for 'the lost.' Romans 1:18–20, *'The wrath of God is being revealed from heaven against all the godlessness and wickedness of men who suppress the truth by their wickedness, since what may be known about God is plain to them, because God has made it plain to them. For since the creation of the world God's invisible qualities — his eternal power and divine nature — have been clearly seen, being understood from what has been made, so that men are without excuse.'* Here, Paul answers a common objection. How could a loving God send anyone to hell, especially someone who has never heard about Christ? In fact, says Paul, God has revealed Himself plainly in the creation of nature and human beings, yet people reject even this basic knowledge of God.

14. We are experiencing the continued outworking of Adam and Eve's sinful rebellion against our Creator that led to a 'broken' world into which we have 'invited' sickness and death. We (humanity) cannot be relieved of our culpability in damaging God's creation, in the same manner as Adam and Eve began, and were warned by God this damage would be the consequence of sin.

15. Everyone has an inner moral sense of what God requires but many choose not to live up to it. Part of this inner sense is explained in Ecclesiastes 3:11, *'He* (God) *has made everything beautiful in its time. He has also set eternity in the hearts of men; yet they cannot fathom what God has done from beginning to end.'* Almost all of us have within a desire to live forever. Both believers and unbelievers will indeed see eternity and appear on

Judgement Day, when the Lord will decide our destiny: as believers we can claim that it is by faith in Jesus that we have been saved (Ephesians 2:8).

16. Covid has resulted in an increased fear of death. However, Christ warns us not to fear death. Luke 12:4–5, '*I tell you, my friends, do not be afraid of those who kill the body and after that can do no more. But I will show you whom you should fear: fear him, who after the killing of the body, has power to throw you into hell.*' Often, we cling to peace and comfort, even at the cost of our walk with God. Jesus reminds us here that we should fear God, who controls eternal, not merely temporal matters.

17. To conclude — whether God gave the Devil permission to send this pandemic, or whether God sent it for His own purpose, either way, He will have His plan. Surely our task is to petition God to fulfil His Covid plan as soon as possible, so that He can then remove the pandemic, which has brought about so much suffering. As this has been a world pandemic, it is possible that once removed, God will herald in a world revival.

Chapter 15
Christian Counselling

How to become a Christian

1. In Acts 1:4–5 Jesus told His disciples that after He ascended to heaven, the Holy Spirit would be sent to the disciples. In fact, this happened ten days after Jesus' ascension, at Pentecost, when many people were amazed at seeing tongues of fire descend on the disciples, as well as other demonstrations of the power of God. The apostle Peter then addressed the crowd of Jewish unbelievers, explaining the reason for Christ's death and resurrection. As Peter was speaking, the crowd was challenged and 'cut to their hearts' by the Holy Spirit.

2. We pick up this event with the last few words of Peter's sermon, Acts 2:36–41: *'Therefore let all Israel be assured of this: God has made this Jesus, whom you crucified, both Lord and Christ. When the people heard this, they were cut to the heart and said to Peter and the other apostles, "Brothers, what shall we do?" Peter replied, "**Repent** and be **baptised**, every one of you, in the name of Jesus Christ for the forgiveness of your sins. And you will **receive the gift of the Holy Spirit.** The promise is for you and your children and for all who are far off — for all whom the Lord our God will call." With many other words he warned them; and he pleaded with them, "Save yourselves*

from this corrupt generation." Those who **accepted his message** *were baptised, and about three thousand were added to their number that day.'*

3. This passage comes at the end of the first New Testament Church sermon and outlines the **four elements** (in bold above) **involved in becoming a Christian**:

1) <u>Verse 38</u>. Peter told the crowd that they had to '**repent**.' If you want to become a Christian, the first thing to understand is that we are all sinners. Romans 3:23, *'all have sinned and fall short of the glory of God.'*

I.   Sin makes us 'unclean' so that we cannot approach the Holy God. Some believe that they will be accepted by God because of their 'good life,' but this is the wrong way to approach God, as our best efforts are still infected with sin.

II.   When Adam sinned, it was as if sin became part of humanity's DNA. Therefore, our only hope of being saved is through repentance and faith in the sacrificial death of Jesus Christ, who enabled us to turn away from sin towards Christ — seeking His forgiveness, mercy, guidance and purpose.

2) <u>Verse 41</u>. *'Those who **accepted his message'**,* or in other words, 'those who believed,' the message of the good news about Jesus. In Mark 1:15, Jesus said, *"The kingdom of God is near. Repent and believe the good news!"*

I.   To 'believe' is more than intellectual agreement that Jesus is God. It means to place our full trust and confidence in Him that He alone can save us. It is to put Christ in charge of our present plans and eternal destiny.

II.   Believing is both trusting his words as reliable and relying on Him for the power to change. Repentance and belief in Christ results in eternal life in Christ.

3) <u>Verse 38</u>. Peter told the crowd '*to repent and be baptised.*' Baptism identifies us with Christ and with the community of believers. It is a condition of discipleship and a sign of faith. John 4:1, '*Jesus was gaining and baptising more disciples than John.*'

4) <u>Verse 38</u>. '*And you will* **receive the gift of the Holy Spirit.**' As humans we have a body, soul and spirit. The body and soul primarily relate to things on earth, whilst the spirit is able to relate to God. However, in unbelievers the spirit is in a deep coma, or sleep — unresponsive to God.

I.   John 3:7–8 (Jesus said), "*You must be born again. The wind blows wherever it pleases. You hear its sound, but you cannot tell where it comes from or where it is going. So, it is with everyone born of the Spirit.*"

II.   Being 'born again' does not reform, but rather regenerates a person, whose spirit becomes alive and responsive to God. Born again believers have the privilege of getting to know and love God.

III.   John 14:17 (Jesus said), '*He* (the Holy Spirit) *lives with you* (that means that when we are 'born again' the Holy Spirit is with us) *and will be in you.*' Some Christians think that at some stage after new birth the Lord may baptise a believer <u>in</u> the Holy Spirit. When this happens the Lord's power is manifested dramatically in the believer, who is empowered and equipped for service and ministry.

Counselling an enquirer after the Talk

4. Suggested matters to discuss with the enquirer. If you earnestly want to be 'born again', would you like to repent of your sins now and ask Jesus into your life as your Lord and Saviour? If you do, please think over your life, in regard to how through disobedience you have hurt God, who wants to be reconciled with you. We will spend some time in quietness, as you think about how you have rebelled against God.

1) I will then go through a prayer, which you can say after me. At one point in the prayer, I will stop to suggest that you apologize to God, preferably do this silently, identifying your sins, without going into detail, as God will know them anyway.

2) Let us pray, **"Lord Jesus, I know I am a sinner. I believe that You died to bring me forgiveness of sins."** (Stop, and say to the enquirer — 'Please now feel free to apologize silently to God in the way I have just described — then we will continue to pray'). **"Right now, I turn from my sins and open the door of my heart to you. Please forgive my sins and come into my life to be my Lord and Saviour. Thank you for your love for me. Amen."**

3) How do you feel after that prayer? It may have been difficult reliving some of the distressing events in your life. You have asked God to forgive you — He is a merciful God, who wants to forgive those who earnestly repent of their sins and turn to the Lord.

4) You might find the Lord leading you to apologize to those you have wronged. He may also encourage you to repair broken relationships, especially with members of

your family, or those with whom you have had a close relationship.

5) A Christian gets to know God through prayer and praise, sharing one's faith with others, studying the Bible and regularly attending church services, especially the Holy Communion.

6) When, and if, you subsequently sense the Lord has come into your life, enquire from the minister of your church about adult baptism in water.

7) If the Lord has saved you, it will become apparent in your spirit — this will be the start of an eternal, personal relationship with the Lord Jesus Christ. In order to understand some of the changes experienced by ex-prisoners as a result of salvation, read their testimonies in my book, *Freedom in Christ* (chapters 9–14), published by Olympia Publishers.

8) Early in your Christian life, if you want to grow closer to Jesus, ask God to baptise you in the Spirit and hopefully in time you will experience this baptism, which is a kind of endorsement of your faith, equipping you with power for whatever ministry He has prepared for you.

Chapter 16
Counselling a Believer in the Baptism of the Holy Spirit

1. <u>Scriptural Authority for this type of Baptism</u>
1) <u>Christ's Words about the difference of the Holy Spirit being *with* and *in* believers.</u> John 14: 16–17, '*And I will ask the Father, and he will give you another Counsellor to be with you forever — the Spirit of truth. The world cannot accept him, because it neither sees him nor knows him. But you know him, for he lives <u>with</u> you and will be <u>in</u> you.*' At 'new birth' the Holy Spirit comes onto a believer and is <u>with</u> that believer. At a later stage the Holy Spirit may come <u>into </u>a believer — this is called, 'the baptism in the Holy Spirit.'

2) When we first become Christians, as a result of being spiritually 'born again,' the Holy Spirit is very much involved with this experience. However, a number of Christians believe that at some later stage, there is a type of spiritual confirmation by God, when Christ may baptize the believer in the Holy Spirit.

3) <u>Christ explains how the baptism in the Holy Spirit would happen after His glorification.</u> John 7:37–39, '*On the last and greatest day of the Feast, Jesus stood and said in a loud voice, "If anyone is thirsty, let him come to me and drink. Whoever believes in me, as the Scripture has said, streams of living water will flow from within him." By this*

he meant the Spirit, whom those who believed in him were later to receive. Up to that time the Spirit had not been given, since Jesus had not yet been glorified.'

4) Christ's Words to his disciples, who were believers, about what they should do in order to receive the baptism in the Holy Spirit. Acts 1:4–5, *'On one occasion, while he was eating with them, he gave them this command: "Do not leave Jerusalem, but wait for the gift my Father promised, which you have heard me speak about. For John baptised with water, but in a few days you will be baptised with the Holy Spirit."'* (In place of the word, 'with,' the Amplified Bible states, *'Placed in, introduced into — the Holy Spirit'*).

5) It is probable that most of the apostles eventually believed when, after Jesus was resurrected, He appeared to them in a locked room (John 20:21), *'Again, Jesus said, "Peace be with you! As the Father has sent me, I am sending you." And with that he breathed on them and said, "Receive the Holy Spirit..."'* In the above passage Jesus said that in a few days' time they would be baptised with the Holy Spirit. In fact, it was fifty days after most of them had probably been born again that at Pentecost they were baptised in the Spirit in a very dramatic way and were empowered to witness.

6) Christ's Words about the Purpose of the Baptism in the Holy Spirit. Acts 1:8, *'But you will receive power when the Holy Spirit comes on you; and you will be my witnesses in Jerusalem, and in all Judea and Samaria, and to the ends of the earth.'* The purpose of this baptism is to receive power to witness and serve: it also provides believers with a greater assurance in their personal faith.

2. Examples of this Baptism

1) Disciples. Acts 2:1–4, *'When the day of Pentecost came, they were all together in one place. Suddenly a sound like the blowing of a violent wind came from heaven and filled the whole house where they were sitting. They saw what seemed to be tongues of fire that separated and came to rest on each of them. All of them were filled with the Holy Spirit and began to speak in other tongues as the Spirit enabled them.'* This is the fulfilment of Christ's prophecy — see paragraph 1.3 above.

2) Paul. Act 9 relates the dramatic conversion of Paul and how three days later, a disciple in Damascus, called Ananias, was directed by God to meet Paul. Acts 9:17–18, *'Then Ananias went to the house and entered it. Placing his hands on Saul, he said, "Brother Saul, The Lord — Jesus, who appeared to you on the road as you were coming here — has sent me so that you may see again and be filled with the Holy Spirit." Immediately, something like scales fell from Saul's eyes, and he could see again. He got up and was baptised, and after taking some food, he regained his strength.'* Three days after Paul's conversion, he was baptized in the Holy Spirit after Ananias prayed for Paul to be filled with the Holy Spirit, which happened, and his sight was restored.

3) Samaritans. Act 8:12, *'But when they believed Philip as he preached the good news of the Kingdom of God and the name of Jesus Christ, they were baptised, both men and women.'* Acts 8:14–17, *'When the apostles in Jerusalem heard that Samaria had accepted the word of God, they sent Peter and John to them. When they arrived, they prayed for them that they might receive the Holy Spirit,*

because the Holy Spirit had not yet come upon any of them;
they had simply been baptised into the name of the Lord
Jesus. Then Peter and John placed their hands on them, and
they received the Holy Spirit.'

3. <u>Counselling Process</u>

1) Go through scriptures (above).

2) Ask the person being counselled to testify about his conversion with the change that God has brought about as a result of 'new birth.' It will be necessary for the counsellor to have peace about the person's profession of faith before praying for baptism in the Holy Spirit as this is only available for believers — it is like a spiritual confirmation which is available at God's discretion.

3) Remind the person about John 7:37–38 (paragraph 1.3 above) in which Christ said that it was necessary to 'thirst' for this baptism. The problem for many believers is that they are unaware of the availability of this extra dimension of the equipping power of the Spirit, therefore hitherto have not earnestly sought this baptism.

4) Providing the person wants to continue, remind him of Psalm 66:18, *'If I had cherished sin in my heart, the Lord would not have listened and heard my voice in prayer.'* If there is unconfessed sin it is useless praying to God, because 'He will not hear me.' The person being counselled should repent of his sins before proceeding.

5) Explain that while we can pray for baptism in the Spirit, it is the Lord who decides whether or not to provide this.

6) Remind the person of Acts 8:17, *'Then Peter and John placed their hands on them, and they received the*

Holy Spirit.' Ask if it is all right to lay hands on him while praying.

7) If nothing appears to happen, then presumably it is not the Lord's timing. This should not, however, deter the person from continuing to request baptism in the Spirit.

8) If the person is baptized after being prayed for, it is usually a dramatic and illuminating experience, sometimes accompanied by signs, such as 'speaking in tongues.'